♀FF THE WALL

WALL

COMPILED BY RACHEL BARTLETT

PROTEUS BOOKS
LONDON AND NEW YORK

PROTEUS BOOKS IS AN IMPRINT OF
THE PROTEUS PUBLISHING GROUP

UNITED STATES
PROTEUS PUBLISHING CO, INC
733 THIRD AVENUE
NEW YORK. N.Y. 10017

Distributed by
THE SCRIBNER BOOK COMPANIES, INC.
597 FIFTH AVENUE
NEW YORK. N.Y. 10017

UNITED KINDOM
PROTEUS (PUBLISHING) LIMITED
BREMAR HOUSE
SALE PLACE
LONDON W2 1PT

ISBN 0 86276 046 1

FIRST PUBLISHED IN U.S 1982
FIRST PUBLISHED IN U.K 1982.

Copyright 1982 Proteus (Publishing) Group.

EDITOR   Nicky Hodge
DESIGN   JOHN GORDON
DESIGN ASSITANTS   Mandy AND Joss
PRINTED BY   Printer Industria Grafica sa
             Barcelona, Spain
             D.L.B. 28499 - 1982

Acknowledgements

The editor would like
to thank Rachel Bartlett
for her relentless pursuit of
suitable graffiti, Connie Jude
for her cover and inside
illustrations, Carel Moiseiwitsch
for her photographs and
John Gordon and Mandy
for their design and layout.

WOMENS AID TAKES YOU THROUGH THE UPS AND DOWNS

JESUS WAS A TYPICAL MAN — THEY ALWAYS SAY THEY'LL COME BACK BUT YOU NEVER SEE THEM AGAIN

WHAT GOOD IS A PENIS FOR EXCEPT FOR BEING HANDY FOR PEEING WHEN HITCH HIKING

THE FUTURE IS FEMALE ♀

NUKES FADE YOUR GENES

TIDE IS BETTER

EVERY TIME I SEE HIM MY KNEES TURN TO JELLY IS IT LOVE OR IS IT FEAR?

You have to kiss a lot of toads before you find a prince

YEAH, NOT TO MENTION THE WARTS YOU GET IN THE MEANTIME.

LIFE IS A QUESTION OF MIND OVER MATTER—I DON'T MIND AND YOU DON'T MATTER

NO WONDER I'M CONFUSED ONE OF MY PARENTS WAS A WOMAN AND THE OTHER WAS A MAN

PORN IS THE THEORY. RAPE IS THE PRACTICE

MEN WHO POT WOMEN
ON PEDESTALS
RARELY KNOCK THEM OFF

FEEL SUPERIOR
BECOME A NUN

A GIRL AT 17
IS MUCH MORE
OF A WOMAN
THAN A BOY
OF 17

LOVE IS A MANY GENDERED THING

I think I must be a mushroom — everyone FEEDS ME BULLSHIT AND KEEPS ME in the dark.

If the cap fits wear it

EVERY GAY PERSON IS THE PRODUCT OF A HETROSEXUAL RELATIONSHIP

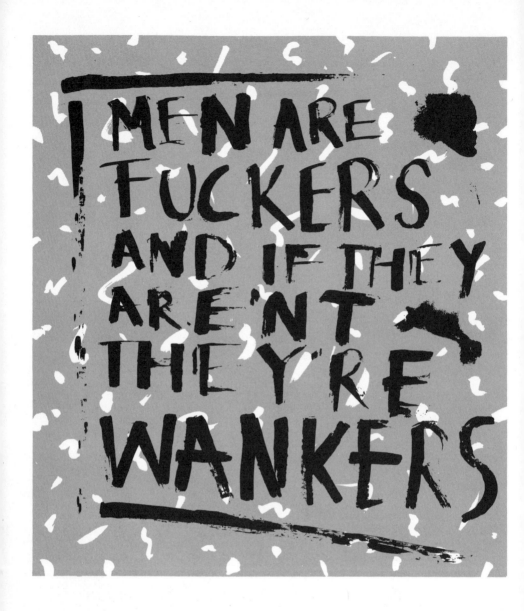

SHOW ME A MAN WHO
SMILES AT DEFEAT
AND I'LL SHOW YOU
A HAPPY CHIROPODIST

THIS DOOR WILL
SHORTLY BE BROADCAST ON
RADIO 4 "WOMAN'S HOUR"

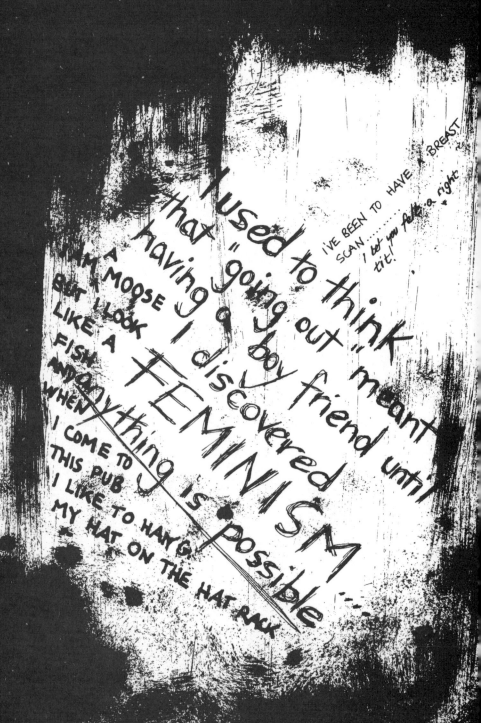

I AM A WOMAN MEANT
FOR A MAN BUT I NEVER
FOUND A MAN WHO COULD
COMPETE

MUMMY, MUMMY, WHAT'S AN ORGASM?
I DUNNO ASK YOUR FATHER

A WOMAN. WHO STRIVES TO BE LIKE A MAN LACKS AMBITION

I THOUGHT CUNNILINGUS WAS AN IRISH AIRLINE UNTIL I DISCOVERED SMIRNOFF

EVERY MOTHER IS A WORKING MOTHER

TO BE
SUCCESSFUL
AT ANYTHING
A WOMAN HAS
TO BE TWICE
AS GOOD AS
A MAN . . .
LUCKILY THIS IS
NOT DIFFICULT.

THIS TOILET'S SO COLD I'M
FREEZING MY ASSETS

ALL AVAILABLE CONTRACEPTION
PUTS THE BURDEN OF
RESPONSIBILITY ON
WOMEN, THE THE TROUBLE
IS WOULD YOU WANT TO
TRUST A MAN TO BE
THAT RESPONSIBLE?

MORE WOMEN
TRAIN DRIVERS—
A WOMAN'S RIGHT
TO CHOO CHOOSE.

EQUALITY IS MAKING HIM SLEEP IN THE WET PATCH

FALLING IN LOVE IS JUST ONE OF LIFE'S PITFALLS

Women reclaim the night

MEN ARE LIKE
ROAST CHICKEN...
THE WHITE BITS ARE THE BEST

SEX with men is
a load of old BALLS

WOMENS AID -
The AFFECT Is SHATTERING.

ADAM TURNED OVER
A NEW LEAF WHEN
HE MET EVE

SEXISM BEGINS AT HOME AND PROLIFERATES IN BARS

I'm on a seafood diet whenever I see food I eat it.

GIRLS ARE POWERFUL

A LITTLE
YEARNING
IS A
DANGEROUS
THING

Woman was Born
FREE but
everywhere is found
in chains.

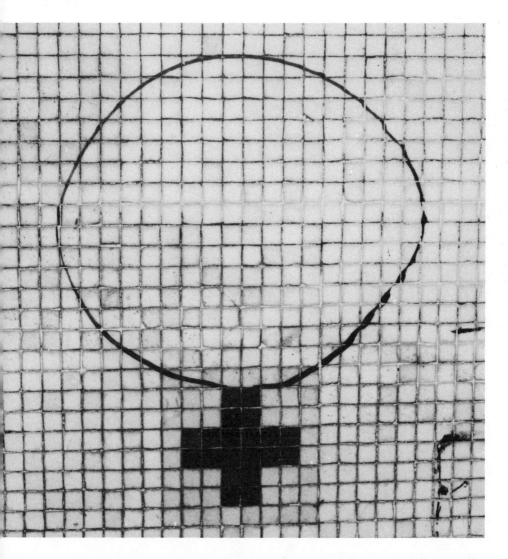

STOP PULLING OUR LEGS

FASHIONS DEFORMS OK.

YOUR NEXT WONDERBRA
WILL DO EVEN MORE FOR YOU
THAN YOUR FIRST...

ossy 15 denier

TAKE
THE TOYS
FROM THE
BOYS

A WOMAN'S
PLACE IS
IN THE
FRONT.

FEMINISM
IS THE THEORY
LESBIANISM
IS THE
PRACTICE

DUDLEY MOORE IS
A PHALLIC THIMBLE

IF YOU EVER
HAD ELEPHANTIASIS
YOU'LL NEVER
FORGET IT.

WICKED WITCHES
WERE INVENTED BY
FRIGHTENED MEN

When God
created
man She
was only
experimenting

(YEAH ADAM WAS A ROUGH DRAFT.)

CUNNILINGUS IS A TONGUETWISTER

GOD CREATED WOMAN IN HER OWN IMAGE

IF THATS A TAMPON
BEHIND MY EAR
WHERE THE FUCK
IS MY PENCIL?

Why does the Pope
wear his underpants in the bath
Because he hates to see th
UNEMPLOYED !

WOMEN HAVE MANY
FAULTS, MEN HAVE ONLY
TWO
EVERYTHING THEY SAY
AND EVERYTHING THEY DO.

INCEST IS A RELATIVE BORE
NECROPHILIA IS A DEAD BORE
CELIBACY IS NEVER BORING

A WOMAN'S
RIGHT TO
REFUSE

A woman without a man
is like a neck without a pain.

IF nothing beats the
great smell of BRUT
then why not use
nothing

HOW DID YOU
FIND YOURSELF
THIS MORNING?
I JUST ROLLED
BACK THE
SHEETS AND
THERE I WAS.

SADISM AND MASOCHISM MEANS NEVER HAVING TO SAY YOU'RE SORRY

MARRIAGE IS A BED OF ROSES. LOOK OUT FOR THE THORNS

RAPE IS AN ACT OF SEXUAL TERRORISM

THOUGHT WANKING WAS PLACE IN CHINA UNTIL DISCOVERED SMIRNOFF

CUNNILINGUS SPOKEN HERE

THAT THE PILL CAN STOP UNWANTED PREGNANCY IS A POPULAR MISCONCEPTION

WHO NEEDS SEXIST ADS? MEN DO TO TRY AND KEEP US IN OUR PLACE

A WOMAN NEEDS A MAN LIKE A FISH NEEDS A BICYCLE

IF SUPERMAN IS SO CLEVER THEN WHY DOES HE WEAR HIS UNDERPANTS ON THE OUTSIDE OF HIS TROUSERS?

LOVE MAKES THE WORLD GO DOWN

BETTER TO HAVE
LOVED AND LOST
THAN TO HAVE
SPENT YOUR
WHOLE DAMN
LIFE WITH HIM

Lesbians
are everywhere...
but not at
the same time

My sister uses
massacre on her eyes

MY MEN FRIENDS
ARE MERELY
THE EXCEPTIONS
THAT PROVE
THE RULE

VIBRATORS ARE
CHEAP AND LONGER
LASTING THEY
ARE ALWAYS READY
AND NEVER DEMANDING
THEY NEVER WANT TO
KNOW IF YOU HAVE
COME OR CALL YOU
FRIGID IF YOU DON'T
AND THEY DON'T
MAKE YOU PREGNANT
GIVE YOU V.D. OR SNORE.

LL RELATIONSHIPS ARE

IVE AND TAKE ———

OU GIVE, HE TAKES

I THOUGHT SMIRNOFF
WAS EXCITING UNTIL
I DISCOVERED WANKING

BEHIND EVERY
GREAT WOMAN
THERE'S A MAN WHO
TRIED TO STOP
HER

Underneath they're all Lovable

UNDERNEATH WE'RE ALL ANGRY!

In Super

plunging seamfree bra, in white

BOYS MARRY VIRGINS,
MEN MARRY WOMEN

DONT ACCEPT RIDES FROM
STRANGE MEN AND
REMEMBER ALL MEN ARE
STRANGE AS HELL

DISARM
ALL
RAPISTS

It's not their arms
I'm worried about!

SISTERHOOD IS POWERFUL

IS THERE LIFE AFTER MARRIAGE?

I USED TO HAVE MONEY TO BURN —

MY LOVER WAS THE BEST MATCH

BOTTOM PINCHERS ARE A PAIN IN THE-ARSE

V.D. IS NOTHING TO CLAP ABOUT

THE HAPPIEST DAY OF
MY LIFE WAS WHEN I
DISCOVERED MY
CLITORIS

LOOK CINDERELLA
MAYBE YOU
SHOULD SKIP THE
BALL AND GO TO
THE CONSCIOUSNESS
RAISING GROUP
INSTEAD

WHAT DO YOU CALL TWO
PEOPLE WHO USE THE
RHYTHM METHOD?

PARENTS

A WOMAN NEEDS
A MAN LIKE
A MOOSE NEEDS
A HAT RACK

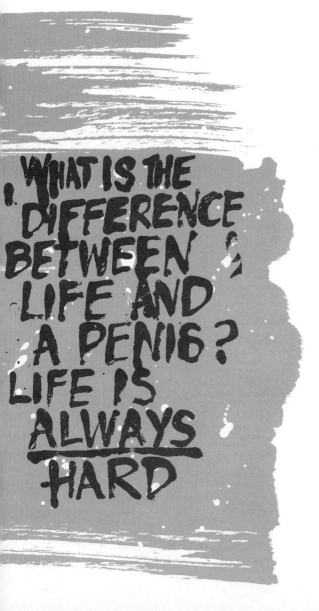

WHAT IS THE
DIFFERENCE
BETWEEN
LIFE AND
A PENIS?
LIFE IS
ALWAYS
HARD

I AM
INTO
BEASTIALITY
SADISM AND
NECROPHILIA...
AM I
FLOGGING A
DEAD HORSE?

RAPE IS VIOLENCE BY THE WEAK AGAINST THE STRONG

WHEN ~~GODIVA~~ WENT FOR HER NAKED RIDE
HER LONG BLONDE HAIR FELL BY HER SIDE
A MENTAL RAPIST TOOK A PEEK
AND WENT CROSSEYED FOR ABOUT A WEEK
(what a shame he didn't drop dead)

EVE WAS THE FIRST
FEMINIST_ SHE TRIED
TO BRING ABOUT THE
FALL OF MAN.

EVERY WOMAN CAN BE A LESBIAN

MY MOTHER MADE ME A LESBIAN

If I gave her the wool will she make me one too?

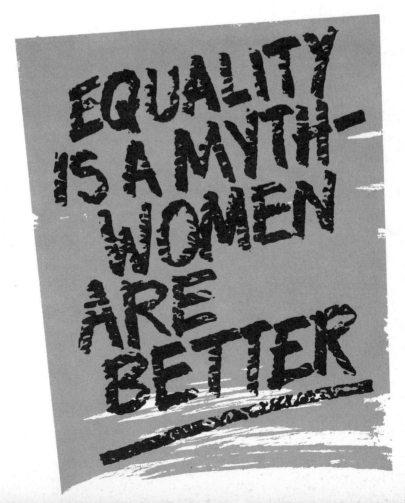

EQUALITY IS A MYTH - WOMEN ARE BETTER

FALLING IN LOVE IS EASY.....
CLIMBING OUT IS THE
DIFFICULT PART.

WHY ARE THE GIRLS KEPT IN WHEN ITS THE BOYS WHO CAUSE ALL THE TROUBLE?

Mini Tampons On Sale
For A Short Period Only!

TO VOLVO, A SON. 4,641 POUNDS

BETTER LUCK NEXT TIME

THE NEW VOLVO 343 HATCHBACK.

IF THIS CAR WAS A LADY IT WOULD GET IT'S BOTTOM PINCHED.

IF THIS LADY WAS A CAR SHE WOULD RUN HIM DOWN!

You can do it in... an M.G

DON'T BORE US WITH YOUR CARS OR YOUR PRICKS

A HOUSE DOES'NT NEED A WIFE ANY MORE THAN IT NEEDS A HUSBAND

A girl's best friends are a girl's best friends

WHEN ALL THAT IS STIFF IS HIS SOCKS TAKE THE MONEY AND RUN

A WOMAN'S PLACE IS IN THE HOME. I WISH I HAD A HOME TO GO TO.

LOVE IS A HEART IN THE HURRICANE OF LIFE!

PENIS ENVY IS JUST A PHALLUSY

SNOOKER FOR WOMEN - A WOMAN'S RIGHT TO CUES.

Y.B.A. WIFE

WIFE

DON'T DO IT DO IT!

MARRIAGE IS A GAMBLE-
HEADS HE WINS, TAILS
YOU LOSE

'IF MEN' GOT PREGNANT ABORTION' WOULD BE A SACRAMENT

SOME DAY MY PRINCE WILL COME, HOWEVER I'LL HAVE NOTHING TO DO WITH IT

WOMEN LIKE THE SIMPLER THINGS IN LIFE - LIKE MEN

A WOMAN'S PLACE IS EVERY PLACE

WHAT'S SO SPEIAL ABOUT CHRISTMAS — THE BIRTH OF A MAN WHO THINKS HE'S A GOD ISN'T SUCH A RARE EVENT!

PARIS EVERY SPRING
JEANS EVERY WEEKEND
DAILY MAIL EVERY DAY
VALIUM EVERY NIGH

I became a feminist as an alternative to becoming a masochist.

WHY IS NOTHING BEING DONE ABOUT APATHY?

WHAT ARE MEN
GOOD FOR?
SCREWING

BEWARE JACK COUSTEAU,
FILMING

Why is that girl trying to pick up my girlfriend?

IF IGNORANCE IS BLISS THEN MEN HAVE REACHED NIRVANA.

WAR IS MENSTRUATION ENVY.

STOP CHATTING ME UP I'M DEAF

Lesbians
IGNITE!

DON'T USE OUR BODIES TO SELL YOUR PRODUCTS

KEEP MY BODY OFF YOUR AD.

HAWAIIAN TROPIC

KEEP IT DA

WHY IS A PRICK
LIKE A ROCKET?
BECAUSE
AFTER IT GOES
OFF YOU SEE
IT GETTING
SMALLER AND
SMALLER

HOW DO LESBIANS
DO IT?

DIFFERENTLY

HOW DARE
YOU PRESUME
I AM HETROSEXUAL

DON'T FAKE ORGASMS OR HE'LL NEVER LEARN TO GIVE YOU ONE

THE BEST THING IS NOT TO LOVE ANYONE EXEPT YOURSELF, THAT WAY YOU CAN SURVIV

I LOST MY VIRGINITY LAST NIGHT - ALL I'M LEFT WITH IS THE BOX IT CAME IN.

MEN ARE THE REAL ENEMY

IT STARTS WHEN YOU SINK IN HIS ARMS AND ENDS WITH YOUR ARMS IN HIS SINK.

I THOUGHT CLAP WAS A FORM OF APPLAUSE UNTIL I DISCOVERED SMIRNOFF.

STAMP OUT RAPE KEEP MEN OFF THE STREETS

YESTERDAY I THOUGHT I SAW TWO PEOPLE WALKING DOWN THE STREET THEN I REALIZED IT WAS A WOMAN WITH A _MAN_

FEMINISM
WOMEN AGAIN

SELF-DEFENCE IS NO ~~OFFENCE~~

HUMANISM
~~S~~T THE TIDE.

WHY ARE GIRLS CALLED BIRDS?

BECAUSE THEY PICK UP WORMS

AN ENGLISHMAN'S HOME IS HIS CASTLE SO LET HIM CLEAN IT.

I JUST SAID NO AND I DON'T FEEL GUILTY

LESBIANS ARE EVERYWHERE... AND A GOOD THING TOO.

I AM 10" LONG AND 3" WIDE.

YES BUT HOW BIG IS YOUR PRICK?